*Easy Devotions to Give*

# Easy Devotions to Give

## Amy Bolding

BAKER BOOK HOUSE

Grand Rapids, Michigan 49506

ISBN: 0-8010-0794-1

*Second printing, November 1981*

Copyright 1980
by Baker Book House Company

*Printed in the United States of America*

# Contents

1. New Every Morning .................................................... 1
2. Frustrations .......................................................... 4
3. Conquest ............................................................. 7
4. God's Timetable ..................................................... 10
5. Power of Attorney ................................................... 13
6. God Is Real .......................................................... 15
7. Promises of Life ..................................................... 18
8. Involved in Life ...................................................... 21
9. What Do You See? .................................................... 24
10. A Journey We All Take ............................................... 28
11. Reduced Prices ...................................................... 30
12. Bright Moments ..................................................... 32
13. An Important Question .............................................. 35
14. Pedaling but Not Going ............................................. 37
15. Idle Tongues ........................................................ 40
16. Your New Year ....................................................... 42
17. Love (Valentine's Day) .............................................. 45
18. Easter Is a Time to Believe ......................................... 49
19. Mothering Is a Full-time Job (Mother's Day) ...................... 52
20. Thanksgiving Miracles .............................................. 55
21. Day of Wonder (Christmas) .......................................... 58

# 1

# *New Every Morning*

*It is of the Lord's mercies that we are not consumed, because his compassions fail not. They are new every morning: great is thy faithfulness. —Lam. 3:22, 23*

One night last week I went to bed feeling that the world had turned its back on me. The postman had failed to bring a desired letter; my head ached; snow covered the ground.

The next morning I awoke to bright sunshine. The snow looked beautiful, and I felt great.

That is typical of our Christian life. There are times when everything seems to go wrong, and we feel there is no way out. Who is at fault? Not God. He gives us new life, new blessings, new mercies every morning.

When the Israelites were hungry in the wilderness, God sent them manna from heaven. They were instructed to gather only the amount they would need each day for their families (Exod. 16:16–18). Exodus 16:21 says, "And they gathered it every morning, every man according to his eating."

Isn't it great that when we go to bed at night we can rest

assured we will have fresh blessings in the morning? God did not promise any of us daily cake, only daily food. When we read our newspapers and watch the news on television, we should realize how much more cake most of us have than the rest of the world.

Martin Luther once said, "Even to feed the sparrows, God spends more than the revenues of the King of France." We are God's children, paid for with the blood of Christ. How much more He cares for us than the sparrows. But so often we fail to see the gifts of God, fresh every morning.

Psalm 104:23 says, "Man goeth forth unto his work and to his labor until the evening." The happiest people are those who have something to do, go and do it, and come home to rest in God's love and protection through the night. They receive fresh strength in the morning.

God is not sitting on His throne to watch and criticize. He is watching to help and love. He knows when the day grows weary and our cares are too much. He is ready to renew our strength.

A college senior had finished the last of several job interviews. He was well trained and ready, but waiting for a job was almost too much for him. His grandfather said, "Son, leave it in God's hands; you have done your best. Now relax and wait." Sure enough, within just a few days the young man received the coveted offer of a good job when he finished school. New mercies come from God each morning.

A bride of one year asked a woman who had just celebrated her fiftieth wedding anniversary, "How did you manage to stay together so long?"

"When you awake each morning, forget the hurts or frustrations of the day before; start fresh with a smile and a kiss," the older woman replied.

Each day we need to see God anew. We need to feel how He loves and cares for us.

## TODAY

Today is ours—let's live it.
And love is strong—let's give it.
A song can help—let's sing it.
And peace is dear—let's bring it.
The past is gone—don't rue it.
Our work is here—let's do it.
The world is wrong—let's right it.
If evil comes—let's fight it.
The road is rough—let's clear it.
The future is vast—don't fear it.
Is faith asleep?—let's wake it.
Today is ours—let's take it.

*Unknown*

# 2

# *Frustrations*

*When I would comfort myself against sorrow, my heart is faint in me.—Jer. 8:18*

*Is there no balm in Gilead; is there no physician there?—Jer. 8:22*

One of the most frustrating things in life is waiting! Waiting for a promised visit, waiting for a special day like Christmas, waiting for a report from the doctor.

Young people often get frustrated waiting for a raise. One of my dearest young friends was so discouraged with his job that he went to another company and interviewed. He was offered a place, no better than the one he had, so he asked for a few days to think it over. He decided to stay where he was. Two months later his boss called him in and gave him a big raise. He would have lost that if he had changed companies and started over.

Like Jeremiah in the above Scriptures, we all feel our hearts faint within us at times. We are as frustrated as he was. Jeremiah tried hard to follow God's instructions, but suffered in doing so and saw little results from his work.

Years ago I knew a young mother with her first baby. She read books on child care, she took him to Sunday school, she saw that he had just the right food. When Billy was ready for school her life became one frustration after another. He stayed after school and got into fights; he scuffed his shoes and tore his sweaters.

This mother always loved her son and bragged on his grades. She saw that he sat by her in church each Sunday. When Billy was a teenager, being a scout kept him on the right track. Years later this mother's dreams came true—Billy was a successful man. He was a leader and a son to be proud of.

When we feel frustration because things fail to go just as we think they should, we can do several things.

Some people just sit and cry and quit trying. They forget God has charge of the timetable. Jeremiah the prophet talks about sitting down and weeping (9:1). Sit down and cry if you have to; a good cry is sometimes what we need, but don't keep on crying. Ask God to take over and give you grace to bear the disappointment.

Others run from their problems. They jump from one location to another, changing jobs and schools. But change is not usually the answer to our frustrations. We take our basic natures with us, so we find problems where we relocate.

Many people do just what Billy's mother did. They go on doing what they feel is best and in the long run the good triumphs.

The greatest thing we can do when we are frustrated is to trust in God, asking Him to fit the pieces of our life together and to show us the way.

When my husband retired we joined two clubs which each met for a potluck dinner once a month. I became frustrated because I did not know how to make fancy salads, so I got out my cookbooks and started to study and experiment. Soon people were saying nice things about my dishes. Frustration made me improve.

Frustrations can ruin your days or they can be pushed aside and forgotten. If you will learn a few good Scriptures and practice saying them silently or aloud when troubled, they will help.

When I am afraid in traffic or at night, I often say Psalm 56:3: "What time I am afraid, I will trust in thee."

When things seem to be completely wrong for me, I think of Romans 8:28: "And we know that all things work together for good to them that love God, to them who are the called according to his purpose." I believe in God, so I claim His promises. I find those promises true and unfailing.

### FOOLISH HEART

Be still my foolish, anxious heart;
　　Why for some greener pastures pine?
Just look around and you will start
　　To recognize your own gold mine!

Be still, and count how blest you are,
　　How much God has done for you.
Why be ungrateful and thus mar
　　Your life and all that you can do?

So many have no pasture green;
　　Their lives are bleak, and dullish gray,
But you some joy can help them glean
　　And make your own a brighter day.

Be still my foolish, anxious heart,
　　And trust the Lord of life today,
For He will help you as you chart
　　Your course and needs for each new day.
　　　　　　　　　　　　　　*J. T. Bolding*

# 3

# Conquest

*Behold, I have set the land before you: go in and possess the land which the Lord sware unto your fathers.—Deut. 1:8*

As Canaan was set before the Israelites, all of life is set before us. Will we conquer it or let it go unpossessed?

The Israelites looked at the Promised Land but were afraid to go in and possess it. Many people have high ambitions and hopes, yet they are afraid to put out the effort to possess them. For example, during World War II I was left alone with three children to care for. My husband was a chaplain and was sent overseas. He sent us enough money to live on so I did not need to work outside my home.

I had in earlier years attended seminary in Fort Worth, Texas. I lacked about nine months of study to get my degree from that school. My sister, living in Fort Worth, found a house for us to rent and offered to help with the children if I would move there and finish school.

Did I live up to my opportunity? No, I was afraid to

7

move to a larger town. I was afraid to try. Now I see how foolish I was.

Why do we fail in our conquest? The immensity of the task set before us often frightens us.

A youth entering college takes a look at the promised land. He sees better job opportunities, better living conditions, a better future if he is prepared. A well-to-do young lady would not go to college because it "took so long." Her high school friend had no rich father to pay her expenses, yet she determined to get a good education. She worked afternoons and evenings as a receptionist and went to classes between times. Four years seemed to her like a long time, yet it passed. She secured a fine position after graduation; she won in her conquest. The rich girl wasted her time, married and divorced, then wandered about aimlessly.

Toby was five months old. His mother bought him a baby walker. Each day Toby spent some time in the walker. He found all kinds of worlds to conquer as he rolled about. As weeks went by he was put out of the walker and onto the floor. He could not walk but he crawled. Soon he pulled up to chairs, and in time he took a few steps without a walker. If his steps faltered, he crawled a little. Toby had an immediate need: to get about the room. He never thought, "I'll just stay in bed; walking is too hard." The determination of a baby is an example for all of us.

As Christians we often fail to seek to win the lost people about us. They might hurt our feelings or they might refuse to listen; they are giants in a promised land.

Living a Christian life in today's world is an immense task and it is an immediate task, for the life we have is now. God calls us to go out and conquer. We can turn back in fear like the Israelites or we can look out at life and hear the words, "Behold, I have set the land before you."

It is easy to criticize, to quit, or to wait for a better time. Joy and satisfaction come in facing up to the conquest and winning.

## ALONG YOUR WAY

Lift up your eyes, ye merry youth,
  Your chance is passing by.
Your opportunity to be
  God's answer to need's cry.

Prepare yourselves each passing day
  For tasks which lie ahead,
And let God use you in His way,
  As by His will you're led.

Your life can be a blessing great,
  But you must will it to;
With faith in God to work and wait
  To see your dreams come true.

Dear lively ones, do not forget
  Today's part of your life.
Give it your best and you will net
  A victory in your strife.

*J. T. Bolding*

# 4

# God's Timetable

*Take ye heed, watch and pray: for ye know not when the time is.—Mark 13:33*

*But when the fullness of the time was come, God sent forth his Son, made of a woman, made under the law.— Gal. 4:4*

My son teaches in a large university. When he was small I did not take him to the college president and say, "Here is my son; he will be a fine teacher; put him over some classes." There is a time for everything. My boy had to grow into a man. He had to attend several colleges until at last he received his Ph.D. and was given a place as a college professor.

God's time is not man's time, and we often get into trouble because we do not wait on God's timetable, but for some things now is the time. For example, it is always time to pray. I Thessalonians 5:17 reads, "Pray without ceasing."

Ephesians 4:26 gives us God's timetable for ending a quarrel. "Be ye angry, and sin not: let not the sun go down upon your wrath." Now is always the time to right a wrong.

If you have had a misunderstanding with a loved one or a friend, now is the time to sacrifice your pride and say, "I'm sorry."

A father had a misunderstanding with his son. He knew he had been too hard on the boy over a trifle, yet he did not say, "I'm sorry; forgive me." Each week he thought, "There will come just the right time." But the son, working at his after-school job, was killed in an explosion. The father's timetable was not right, for he never made peace with his son, and then it was too late.

Never put off telling a friend or loved one how much you admire and appreciate them. The timetable for that is now. We never know when life will separate us and the time will be too late.

During the last years of my mother's life my husband and I tried to make the four-hundred mile trip to visit her about once each three months. One time after such a visit, my sister called to tell me our mother had died suddenly. Even now, several years later, I wish I had told my mother certain things.

We have no control over God's timetable. There is a time to share burdens and a time to share joy. If we are close to God, He lets us know when the right time is.

God waited for just the right time to send Christ into the world (Gal. 4:4). Before that time came, people had been saved by belief in a Savior to come according to God's plan. Since Christ came, we are saved by faith that He came into the world, died on the cross for our sins, arose from the grave, and is interceding for us in heaven. Many people have failed to be saved and inherit an eternal home because they would not accept God's timetable. Scripture says that "today is the day of salvation."

Man's life is laid in the loom of time
  To a pattern he does not see,
While the weavers work and the shuttles fly
  Till the dawn of eternity.

*Unknown*

### IN HIS OWN TIME

We impatiently go running;
  Back and forth, we rush about,
Seldom noting that our cunning
  Often dumbly leaves God out.

Hastily we make decisions
  Which deserve deep thought and prayer
And forget the Lord's provisions,
  His wise wishes, and His care.

We forget that God's timetable
  Is the one we need to meet;
That there's time and He is able
  To direct our stumbling feet.

Yes, God never has to hurry;
  Does not work by our clock's time;
He will guide us, without worry,
  In His own good easy time.

*J. T. Bolding*

# 5

# Power of Attorney

*O God, thou art terrible out of thy holy places: the God of Israel is he that giveth strength and power unto his people. Blessed be God.—Ps. 68:35*

When my husband was told that he would be sent overseas during World War II, he had an attorney write out a power of attorney for me. I could buy and sell in his name. As it happened, I did buy a home for us while he was away.

God has a power of attorney for each of us if we will accept it. He will give us power to live a dynamic life before the judges who stand and watch our Christian performance. "The God of Israel is he that giveth strength and power unto his people" (Ps. 68:35).

Waiting in the wings at a beauty contest, one very pretty young woman was very nervous about being watched.

Her friend said, "Quit worrying about being watched, just be worthy of being watched."

Most often the prettiest girl in a beauty contest is the one who is unconscious of her beauty and charm. We as Christians often fail to recognize what super people we can be if we will only let the power of God take over in our lives.

Who watches us? All creation. People who are not Christians watch to see if there is anything to our religion. People who long to have a better life want to know how. Your immediate family watches you to see if you do or do not do certain things. Girls in beauty contests are watched only for four or five days, but Christians are watched at all times. We must strive to be worthy of being watched.

When at last my husband returned home from the war, he saw for the first time the house I had bought. He saw the checkbook for the first time in two years. He asked questions, and I gave him an accounting. How happy my husband was to know I had saved some money for the period of time he might have to spend looking for work. How proud he was that we were not in debt and yet had a home. And just as I had to give an account to my husband, the day will come for each person to give an account of his life to God.

God will give us power to live a great and glorious life here under one condition: we must give God the power of attorney to take our lives and use them as He sees best. If we turn our lives over to God there will be power available to us that we never dreamed of.

# 6

# *God Is Real*

*A friend loveth at all times, and a brother is born for adversity.—Prov. 17:17*

*A man that hath friends must shew himself friendly; and there is a friend that sticketh closer than a brother.— Prov. 18:24*

*And the house which I build is great: for great is our God above all gods.—II Chron. 2:5*

When the pastor of a church came back to the pulpit after an illness of four months, he made the following statement: "I may not know what it is to be a friend, but I know what it is to have a friend."

God had been with that man during his hours of illness: he was aware that God was his friend.

When we are sitting on top of the world and life is rosy, we are prone to forget God and His love. But when trouble comes and the world looks black, and we wonder how we can go on, we reach out and hold to God with all our strength.

A friend called us in the dark of night to come quickly;

his child was about to die. Doctors were not sure what terrible disease had struck. As we all knelt in the hospital chapel and prayed fervently for the child, that young father made some promises to God.

Later when the child was well and a joy to his parents, the father was asked to give a testimony in church. In telling of how real God was to him, he made this statement: "There is a personal satisfaction in knowing I have met God's requirements. I never plan to pinch pennies or split hairs with God."

We often are weak Christians because we fail to have the abiding knowledge that God is real and wants what is best for us at all times.

A mother of three sacrificed to buy a good set of encyclopedias for her children. Over and over they studied those books as they worked on school assignments. The mother felt the books were well worth what they cost, because all her children made good grades by becoming friends with the encyclopedias.

Do you know a great old Christian, whose path you know has at times been very rough, yet the person is calm, serene, and happy? That person has made friends with Jesus, the friend who sticks closer than a brother.

Our God is real and exciting! It is wonderful to know that God created all things and knows all things, yet He knows us intimately and wants to help when we have need, to rejoice with us when we have blessings, to mourn with us when our hearts are torn asunder with grief. God is not made of stone or wood to set on a shelf. He is a spiritual being, all powerful and great, and He is our friend.

## STRENGTH

Oft I'm discouraged and slothful,
  Utterly failing each day,
And my poor life is so prayerless
  That I need strength just to pray.

Surely I know life's a battle;
  I chose the side of the right,
And I must ever press onward
  In this continuous fight.

Thank you, dear Lord, for your presence,
  Giving to me strength to win
Victory through thy salvation
  Over the power of sin.

Thank you, dear Lord, for your Spirit,
  Walking beside me each day,
Bringing me comfort and blessings
  Every step of the way.

*J. T. Bolding*

# 7

# Promises of Life

*Whereby are given unto us exceeding great and precious promises.—II Peter 1:4*

When I was a young mother with three small children, I would sometimes ride the streetcar to downtown Fort Worth to go shopping. The children would remain at home with an aunt. Always as I left I promised to bring them back a surprise. The dime store was usually my first stop, and I selected a small toy for each child. Then I went about buying a few things for myself.

When the streetcar stopped in front of our house on my return, my three children ran to meet me, shouting, "Did you get the surprise?"

Jesus gives us some great and precious promises when we give our hearts to Him. He will keep those promises.

A plane carrying twelve forest rangers went down in a body of water, killing most of the men. One of the youngest, nineteen years old, managed to get to shore. He felt there was a promise of rescue and help a few miles away. Before he found anyone to help he had walked ten miles. The hope and promise of help kept him going.

Many times in life we feel our world has crashed about us, but the love and promises of God keep us going until we turn the corner and life is bright again.

When we give our hearts to Jesus we select a friend for life. Christ is a friend that "sticketh closer than a brother" (Prov. 18:24). What a joy it is at the close of a long day to talk over our day with a friend. Christ is always available through prayer. The Holy Spirit will help direct and impress us with the way we should go.

We not only have the promise of friendship with Christ, but we have fellowship with other Christians as well.

A friend recently went to the hospital for a simple operation on her leg, but the pathology report after the operation was discouraging. The doctors were sure there was cancer someplace else in her body. Her Sunday school class sent flowers, friends sent cards, and people visited her in the hospital.

"I didn't know how wonderful Christian friends were until this happened," she said.

Christ has promised many things. He promised a comforter for our sorrows. He promised to take our prayers and petitions to the heavenly Father. He promised to return to earth, to prepare us a home, to be ever with us. All these promises and many more He will keep. We need have no fear.

### PROMISES

It's not hard to make a promise
    When a little pressure mounts,
But the keeping isn't easy,
    And the keeping is what counts.

People often are neglectful
  In the keeping of their word
And forgetful of a promise,
  As you possibly have heard,

But the Lord is O so faithful,
  And He never does forget;
For His promises  I'm grateful;
  Yes, He never broke one yet.
                              *J. T. Bolding*

# 8

# *Involved in Life*

*Grace be unto you, and peace, from God our Father, and from the Lord Jesus Christ.—Phil. 1:2*

*I thank my God upon every remembrance of you.—Phil. 1:3*

*Simon Peter, a servant and an apostle of Jesus Christ, to them that have obtained like precious faith with us through the righteousness of God and our Saviour Jesus Christ: Grace and peace be multiplied unto you through the knowledge of God, and of Jesus our Lord.—II Peter 1:2*

The above Scriptures are greetings from Paul and from Peter to the Christian people. These men were involved in telling people about life eternal and how to obtain it.

In your life are you a greeter, or are you a "greetee"? Are you a giver or a taker?

A few years ago, a nice couple in our church gave my husband and me tickets for a trip to the Asian churches. We flew to Athens, Greece. From Athens we boarded a ship, and for fifteen days we went from place to place.

The first ruins we visited were the ruins of Philippi. We could picture a house nearby, where in perhaps the same month (June) of A.D. 62, a group of believers waited for a messenger to arrive, bringing a letter from their beloved Paul. Paul was far away in prison, yet he wanted to be involved in the life of the group of Christians in Philippi.

Paul was a greeter, and his letters were filled with joy and praise. How often we write to a dear friend, wanting to let them know in a special way how much they mean to us. We write, "I thank my God upon every remembrance of you."

There are many greeters in life who do not even realize they are givers. When Sue finished high school, her closest friends were going away to college. Her father was out of work and she had to get a job to help keep the family together. Sue cried bitterly in the fall when her friends left.

"Now look about you," her mother said. "Your daddy will soon get a job and you can still go away to school, or you can get involved in the community and be a leader here at home. Make up your mind and put on a brave front."

Sue put on a smile. Soon she was working and going with a nice young man. A new music director came to her church and he noticed that Sue had a wonderful voice. He started giving her voice lessons, and soon she was singing solos. People started calling Sue when they needed special music. Her young man asked her to marry him. Her life was full and happy because she became involved with helping others. She became a giver, a greeter.

Get involved; be a greeter. Think of each morning as not "just another day" but as a fresh opportunity.

Some people have an unhealthy interest in themselves to the exclusion of those about them. They want attention but don't want to give any to others. For example, one wealthy woman had no friends because she would not be a greeter. She would call up people and say ugly things to them because they hadn't called her. She got angry if she didn't get a birthday card or Christmas card, yet she bragged that she never sent cards.

When I was young I didn't realize how much old people like to get letters telling all about what the children and grandchildren are doing. I wrote my parents and parents-in-law, but I never really took pains to make them see what was happening at our house. Now the shoe is on the other foot. I treasure each letter and each call from the precious ones I call mine.

Take time to share with someone. Your life, as well as the life of the one you take time for, will be enriched.

### ONE-WAY TRIP

There's a malady that brings to nothing
    Many a high and noble thought,
Often leading into desolation,
    Disappointment, and to naught.

Idleness some folks consider pleasure;
    In it, they think they have achieved,
But the worthwhile things they should accomplish,
    Wasted, cannot be retrieved.

Life is just a one-way trip or passage;
    Opportunities don't stay.
Let us make the most of every moment;
    We'll not pass again this way.

*J. T. Bolding*

# 9

# *What Do You See?*

*Say not ye, There are yet four months, and then cometh harvest? behold, I say unto you, Lift up your eyes, and look on the fields; for they are white already to harvest.—John 4:35*

Allen and John were four-year-old boys who lived near each other. They were not allowed to go past the middle of the block alone. A big boy named Joe came to visit in the neighborhood and could find no one his own age to play with. When he found out that Allen and John were not allowed out of the sight of their mothers alone, he went to the door of each and asked if he could walk the boys around the block.

When John came back from the walk and was called in for lunch, his mother asked, "What did you see?"

"A big wild dog," he said. "If Joe hadn't been along, the dog would have eaten us up."

"I believe that dog is kept behind a fence," his mother said.

"Then we saw a mother pushing her baby in a carriage. And later we saw a grandfather, digging in his yard." On and on John went, telling what he had seen on his walk around the block.

His mother was pleased that he had noticed so much.

Allen's mother never bothered to ask him what he had seen; she was wrapped up in a television program and was glad that for a short time she didn't have to be aware that she had a child.

We are on a walk through life, and our heavenly Father is very interested in what we see as we walk along.

Twenty years ago as a Sunday school teacher I often took a class member with me to visit women our age, inviting them to attend our class. We found some who really wanted to get started but were timid. Others we found were in need of financial help. They needed food and clothes for their children.

Now my husband and I visit people who are too old and too sick to attend a church service. They are lonely and feel forgotten and neglected.

We see different things at different ages of life. Jesus told us to look on the fields of people, to see their needs.

I read the story of a very successful businessman. He belonged to a church and attended on Sundays, but, as he worked through the week, he never thought of the people he met as being either lost or saved.

Then a visiting evangelist came to his church and preached on "Seeing Those Around You." The man was made to look on the fields and see the harvest. He went to some of the people he worked with and told them the story of Jesus. He found a number of men ready to go and hear the sermons. Several of his friends trusted in Christ for salvation.

During one night of the revival the man went down the

aisle weeping. The pastor asked him his problem and he said, "I am so ashamed that I have gone so many years without seeing anything about me. I want the lost people to forgive me."

We are responsible for telling the people around us about Jesus. If we don't tell them who will?

One day I stood to bring a devotion to a class of older women. As I looked for a moment at their faces, I realized that they needed to laugh. They looked so lost, so sad.

I told about a dozen jokes and then finished with a serious thought. The teacher called the next day and said she appreciated being made to laugh. We must see the need of those we come in contact with in order to minister to them.

It takes far-seeing people to make the world a better place. Men had to dream about flying before they ever built a plane. Many storms have to be weathered before a dream can come true.

Christian people have to pray before a revival can come. And they have to see a lost world before they care to pray. We need to stop sitting and dreaming and get up and work to make our dreams come true.

What do you see? Is life dull and drab? Are you alone and miserable? Do you see the beauty about you each day as flowers bloom and trees leaf out? God made a beautiful world, but we see only what we look for. If you look for a friend to hurt you, you will be hurt. If you look for a chance to be a blessing, you will see people who need you.

Look at others and not at yourself, then you will begin to be a blessing.

## WHAT DO YOU SEE?

Four months and then comes the harvest,
 Jesus said some folks will say;
But He looked at fields and people
 In a very different way.

Our dear Saviour looked on harvests
 As an every moment thing
Which demands our close attention,
 Summer, winter, fall, and spring.

Life and love and health abiding;
 Friends and blessings, O so dear;
Sweet assurance of salvation:
 Daily harvest of His care.

Blessed, constant, loving, caring:
 God bestows at rapid rate,
Harvests of dear souls and blessings:
 Let us reap; it's growing late.

Souls are lost and men are dying
 Without hope right in our way;
Tell, O tell them that salvation
 Is available today.

*J. T. Bolding*

# 10

# *A Journey We All Take*

*And he said, Let us take our journey, and let us go, and I will go before thee.—Gen. 33:12*

Our Scripture text refers to a journey Jacob was taking back to his home after many years of absence.

The Christian life is often compared to a journey. Our Lord does not want us to sit still except for one thing: "Be still, and know that I am God" (Ps. 46:10).

When we start planning a trip for vacation or for education, we usually think first of who will accompany us—our married partner, our children, a friend?

As Christians we decide to take Christ as our Savior and Lord, as our traveling companion through life. We often make mistakes when we fail to talk over each day with Him our anticipated moves and decisions. Meet with Him each new day to face new experiences, new challenges. There is richer grace to be discovered along the road each day. Always new blessings and new mercies are awaiting us.

If you want a happy journey of life, take along Christ.

Travel with Christian companions. Follow the instructions Christ gave us: Do unto others as you would have them do unto you. Comfort the sick and sad. Give to those in need.

In Scripture we read of the prodigal son, the son of a wealthy rancher who wanted to take his journey to far places. Reluctantly his father gave him his part of the property. With the wrong companions he spent his money and became hungry, ragged, and dirty. He had taken as his companions greed, pleasure, lust. Home looked good to him when he finally came to his senses and returned. His father still loved him, but he had wasted his inheritance.

How many times after a long trip have you stopped the car in your own driveway and said, "This is the most beautiful place we have been since we left"? Much more beautiful will be the sight of the home our heavenly Father has prepared and waiting for us at the end of our earthly journey.

### BUT ONCE

We go this way but once, O heart of mine,
So why not make the journey well worth while,
Giving to those who travel with us
A helping hand, a word of cheer, a smile?

We go this way but once. Ah! never more
Can we go back along the selfsame way,
To get more out of life, undo the wrongs,
Or speak love's words we knew but did not say.

We go this way but once. Then let us make
The road we travel blossomy and sweet
With helpful, kindly deeds and tender words,
Soothing the path of bruised and stumbling feet.

*Unknown*

# 11

# *Reduced Prices*

*No mention shall be made of coral, or of pearls: for the price of wisdom is above rubies.—Job 28:18*

*Christ hath redeemed us from the curse of the law, being made a curse for us: for it is written, Cursed is every one that hangeth on a tree: That the blessing of Abraham might come on the Gentiles through Jesus Christ; that we might receive the promise of the Spirit through faith.—Gal. 3:13, 14*

People flock to stores at the end of the summer when stores get rid of the last of their summer merchandise at reduced prices. Everyone loves a bargain.

But there are some things we should never seek at reduced prices. We are God's highest creation, and He expects us to live above the other created things. When He saw how we were inclined to be sinful and wicked, He asked His Son to pay the very highest price for our redemption (Gal. 3:13, 14). Christ came from heaven's glory and suffered shame, abuse, and death for our redemption. Some people try to buy salvation at a reduced price. They work hard on church committees or give lots of money to a church, but they never turn their hearts over to Jesus.

In Matthew 18:3 Jesus said, "Except ye be converted, and become as little children, ye shall not enter into the kingdom of heaven." Children can do very little for themselves; they must depend on others. We must trust Christ for our salvation. He paid a great price for it, but for us it is free.

A young pastor came to a church. He saw there was much money coming in each Sunday and he took more than his share. The price was too high; he lost his church.

People of all ages try to buy their way through life at reduced prices. Children cheat at school because they think it is easier than learning. Some men and women seek fun and pleasure at reduced prices; they cheat on a companion. But in the long run, many have had to pay a greater price—a broken family, bitterness, and heartache.

Our Scripture text, ". . . the price of wisdom is above rubies," is one every parent should learn and teach to his or her children.

God made us with the potential for greatness, but many of us sell ourselves short. We fail to develop our talents; we skimp at our jobs. Others work hard to make life better. For example, look about your home. If someone had not spent time and effort inventing some of the machines and gadgets you use each day, life would be harder.

When I was young, my grandparents had no refrigerator. Ice was bought about once every two or three weeks and kept in the cellar. Then ice boxes were invented. How great it seemed to have a man bring ice to the house each day. Soon after I married, electric refrigerators were invented.

Someone pays the price in study and work for every new thing. Life is precious; we may accomplish a lot if we refuse to live at reduced prices.

# 12

# *Bright Moments*

*At midday, O king, I saw in the way a light from heaven, above the brightness of the sun, shining round about me and them which journeyed with me.—Acts 26:13*

Have you ever been discouraged and then asked God to send you a blessing? God answers prayer.

God often sent bright moments to his servants in the Bible. One of the best known is when He spoke to Saul on the road to Damascus. Saul's life was completely changed.

Do we use the power we have to shed brightness, to help change people's lives?

Years ago I met a friend in the wholesale jewelry business on the street. He stopped me, and we chatted a moment. Then he took a small string of imitation pearls from his pocket and gave them to me. My friend has been dead for ten years now, but the brightness he shed lingers on in my heart. We all can remember times when someone spread a little brightness in our lives.

Most ministers, including my husband, never make a

great amount of money, yet God never fails to send people to minister to them. A man I did not know rang our door bell one day and handed me a sack filled with fresh garden produce. My day was brighter because someone thought of us.

You do not have to give pearls or produce to brighten someone's day. All you need is a friendly greeting and a smile. When I was a small child, we lived a block from the railroad track, and sometimes Mother would let us go down close to the track to wave at the engineer and fireman. What a thrill! When they waved back, our day was made.

The toddler who lives across the street from us waves at my husband. She brightens his day. To him she is the sweetest baby in town.

Often we miss an opportunity to brighten someone's day; we are so wrapped up in our own problems we fail to encourage and help others. A young girl went to visit her grandmother. She was eager to tell her about a small honor she had received in school. The grandmother merely nodded at the news of the child's accomplishments, then started telling how smart the girl's mother had been in school. The child went away disappointed; the grandmother missed giving the child brightness.

Praise is a great way of spreading brightness. All humans like to be praised. A child will respond to praise and seek to please.

Comfort is also a form of brightening someone's day. Life can look so dark after the loss of a loved one or after a financial loss. A few words of encouragement can help make the world look brighter.

Bright moments are good to give and good to get. A husband especially likes to see a bright and pleasant face at the breakfast table. Things are tough in the working world, and he likes to feel that home is safe and secure.

A family I know always holds hands around the table when they give thanks for their food. This makes mealtime sweet, and touching is reassuring to the whole family.

Bright moments are something you can give to others. They cost nothing except thoughtfulness and effort. Smile at those you meet on the street; speak cheerfully to people you know. Praise your companion. At the close of the day you will be relaxed and happy that you made the effort to brighten the day for others.

### PRECIOUS THING

Your life is such a precious thing,
    And only God could give it,
But you have such a privilege
    For only you can live it.

If problems great beset your soul,
    The Father always loves you;
He has the power to guide and keep,
    And sets a watch above you.

Each day's a treasure for your care,
    With privilege and duty,
With joys and sorrows, pain and peace
    And landscapes bathed with beauty.

It is your privilege to live,
    Today, perhaps tomorrow,
So live in such a blessed way
    As not to cause folk sorrow.

*J. T. Bolding*

# 13

# *An Important Question*

*So when they had dined, Jesus saith to Simon Peter, Simon, son of Jonas, lovest thou me more than these? He saith unto him, Yea, Lord; thou knowest that I love thee. He saith unto him, Feed my lambs.—John 21:15*

Not long ago we spent a night in the home of our oldest granddaughter. She has a three-year-old daughter. When the end of the day came, the child's father came home from work. The little child ran to him to be caught up in strong arms and kissed.

"Do you love me, Pam?" her father asked.

"I love you, Daddy," she replied. He was happy with her answer. Soon the child was playing with her toys again.

Jesus, our great and wonderful Savior asked the same question of his followers. Repeatedly Jesus asked Peter if he loved Him. Then He gave Peter a commission: "Go feed my lambs." Peter loved Jesus, so he spent his life telling the lost about a Savior who died for them.

Love makes us think about the object of our love. A teenager in love keeps the phone busy calling his girlfriend.

When we love someone, we think about that person and we speak about that person. We seek to be near to and we try to please the one we love.

A young man in college fell in love, and he could not take time to go home for a visit until his parents told him to bring his girlfriend with him. Tom's parents were amazed to see how he waited on his lovely sweetheart. Her smallest wish was his command.

A new convert is often like Tom. He seeks to tell others about his new found Savior. He wants to be at church when the doors are opened. He prays and seeks to do what God wants him to do.

I Corinthians 13 is called the love chapter of the Bible. "And now abideth faith, hope, love, these three; but the greatest of these is love" (I Cor. 13:13).

## PEOPLE BRIDGES

Everybody builds some bridges
    Which are thoughts, in word and deed;
Some cross rivers or join ridges
    Just to meet somebody's need.

Bridges take on many natures
    And appear in lots of forms,
Bearing varied nomenclatures,
    Helping quiet people's storms.

Clasped, or waving, or extended,
    Hands may bridge some chasms wide,
So that broken ties are mended
    And men can in peace abide.

Books, ideas, words, and glances,
    Help good hearts search for a way.
Smiles, kind  looks, a thought advances,
    Bridging people gaps each day.

                                        *J. T. Bolding*

# 14

# *Pedaling, but Not Going*

*So shall my word be that goeth forth out of my mouth: it shall not return unto me void, but it shall accomplish that which I please, and it shall prosper in the thing whereto I sent it.—Isa. 55:11*

A small child came to my house one day while I was working very hard at pedaling my exerciser. The child watched awhile, fascinated.

Finally he said, "You are pedaling but not going."

Many times in life we get the feeling we are pedaling but not going. We spin our wheels without moving forward because we don't expect to move; we are content to sit. We forget our main purpose is to tell others about salvation in Jesus Christ.

Icicles form one drop at a time. We can look out the window in the morning and see small slender tapers of ice hanging from the roof. Then a few hours later the same taper of ice will be twice as large and a lot longer. Christian character is formed in much the same way—one thought, one act, one feeling at a time.

In daily living we need to use a bike that will take us places. Many men are failures because they are riding an exerciser in place of a vehicle capable of going places. Men need to rely on the infinite power of God to take them places.

A minister was very burdened about some problems in his church. One day he came home more discouraged than usual. His small son, paralyzed from polio, was all alone in the living room.

"Where is your mother?" the minister asked.

"She had to go work upstairs for a little while."

"I want to give her this package," the father said.

"Oh, Daddy let me give it to her," the child pleaded.

"How can you give it to her when you can't walk?"

"That is easy; you let me hold the package and you carry me up the steps."

As they went up the stairs, tears fell from the man's eyes. "I have been trying to carry all the load. If I will just trust God to lift me up in His arms, I can succeed with my church."

It isn't enough just to be busy. What are you busy doing? It isn't enough for me to pedal on an exerciser; I need to get out and go places, use my legs to walk and accomplish daily living.

It isn't enough just to go to church on Sunday; we need to be working to bring in the kingdom. Satan enjoys seeing Christian people riding an exerciser. He knows they are not winning anyone as long as they are standing still. Sleeping saints serve Satan well.

### LIVE THE WAY YOU PRAY
I knelt to pray when the day was done,
And prayed, "O Lord, bless everyone,

Lift from each saddened heart the pain
And let the sick be well again."
And when I woke another day
And carelessly went on my way,
The whole day long I did not try
To wipe a tear from any eye.
I did not try to share the load
Of any brother on my road.
I did not even go to see
The sick man next door to me.
Yet once more when the day was done,
I prayed, "O Lord bless everyone!"
But as I prayed, into my ear
There came a voice that whispered clear.
"Pause, Hypocrite, before you pray.
Whom have you tried to bless today?
God's sweetest blessings always go
By hands that serve Him here below."
And then I hid my face and cried,
"Forgive me, God, for I have lied,
Let me but live another day
And I will live the way I pray."

*Anonymous*

# 15

# *Idle Tongues*

*But I say unto you, That every idle word that men shall
speak, they shall give account thereof in the day of
judgment.—Matt. 12:36*

A man in our city had cause to regret an idle tongue a
few years ago. After a long plane flight, he was tired and
anxious to get home. A redcap offered to take his bag.

"I'll carry it myself; it's full of bombs," the man said. He
did not mean it at all, but in a few moments he was stopped
by the police, his bag was opened and searched, and he was
taken to the police station and fingerprinted. It was some
time before he was free to go home, all because of an idle
statement.

A mother said some idle words of advice to a young man
who was calling on her daughter. The young man never
came back again. He had enjoyed the company of the girl,
but he resented the mother giving him advice about his job.
The man was proud of his job; he worked hard at it and
expected to advance as time passed.

When we say idle words we not only hurt others, we very often hurt ourselves as well. Idle words or speculation against some person's character often causes irreparable hurt and damage. Idle talk is a bad habit. Some people eat every time they get bored or lonely, others run to a friend's house and start talking. My husband often says, "Stay away from that person. She is like a river; her mouth is open and runs all the time."

We must always weigh the consequences of what we say before we speak. Jesus said that we will have to give an account for every idle word.

# 16

# *Your New Year*

*Delight thyself also in the Lord; and he shall give thee the desires of thine heart. Commit thy way unto the Lord; trust also in him; and he shall bring it to pass.—Ps. 37:4, 5*

Somewhere in some old school notes I found the following poem.

### THE GOLDEN RULE EXEMPLIFIED
Speak no evil and cause no ache
Utter no jest that will pain awake.
Guard your actions and bridle your tongue
For words are adders when hearts are stung.

Help whoever, whenever you can
Man forever needs aid from man.
Never let a day die in the west
That you have not comforted some sad breast.

*Unknown*

As we come face to face with a new year, most of us want to make some contribution to the good of our fellowmen.

Many people make resolutions and never keep them. Others make resolutions and keep them a short while. At any rate, it is better to try and fail than never to try.

Most of us want peace and contentment from life. The very best way to get peace and contentment is to do something each day you live to make happiness for others.

In the neighborhood where I live there are very few houses with gardens. Most of us prefer to have shrubs and flowers. One dear man planted vegetables in his back yard. He gives his friends the tomatoes and beans and other produce from his garden. Often I see this same man sitting on his porch talking to the neighbor children. He seems content.

Another thing we all want for the new year is to make our loved ones happy. A cross, unhappy family will never find contentment unless they change. How shall we accomplish these things? Our Scripture verses give us a beginning point: "Commit thy way unto the Lord; and he shall give thee the desires of thine heart" (Ps. 37:5).

If we commit anything to another we must first trust that person. So as we commit to God we must trust Him. He is our refuge. Through the coming year we will seek and trust that refuge.

A popular tennis player had a heart attack. He said he had observed all the rules for good health. Yet trouble came to him. We can try our best in our own strength to be good and perfect, yet we will fail without the help of God.

We all made some mistakes during the past year, but is it necessary to carry them on our backs all next year? No! Ask forgiveness for the past and start a clean record for the new year.

We were gathering rocks and shells along the shore of the gulf. Many people had been there in days before, and pickings were slim. Looking ahead we saw a large shell—just what we wanted.

"We will put it into our sack last; it will be heavy," we said.

Then a large wave rolled in and quickly out again, carrying with it the big shell we had planned to put in the sack last.

If we are not careful the waves of daily living will wash over our new year and take our plans and resolutions out to sea.

### A HAPPY YEAR

If we would act toward other folk
  As we would have them do,
Just think how great the happiness
  We'd share the whole year through!

If only thoughts of truthfulness
  And words of loving cheer
Escaped our lips, what happiness
  Would visit us each year!

If we ourselves would promise
  To act from motives true,
Each year would be a happy one
  In everything we do.

*Unknown*

# 17

# *Love*

## *(Valentine's Day)*

*And the Lord make you to increase and abound in love one toward another, and toward all men, even as we do toward you.—I Thess. 3:12*

*And now abideth faith, hope, love, these three; but the greatest of these is love.—I Cor. 13:13*

A long time ago in England a Sunday school was making up a box of things to send to a tribe in Africa. In a class of small girls, all except one had a garment to put in. The little girl had barely enough clothes for herself, but she wanted so much to send a gift.

The child told her mother about the project, and the mother said, "You shall not be left out. Here is a penny. Tell your teacher to put it in for you."

The teacher took the penny and bought a gospel tract about the love of Jesus. Proudly the little class put the tract in the very top of the box.

When the box arrived in Africa, the chief's son was the one to open the box. He took the tract for himself and gave away the other things. The young man, a prince in his country, became a Christian from reading the tract. Then he worked to tell the story of Jesus to many others.

All this happened because one child wanted to send what she could to show her love for others.

All kinds of money is spent by governments to develop power, but the greatest power in the world is generated by love—love for one another and love for God. Proverbs 13:7 reads, "There is that maketh himself rich, yet hath nothing: there is that maketh himself poor, yet hath great riches."

How very rich we are when we have love in our homes. Many men and women work so hard at positions for salary, while their children run about without much supervision and get into all kinds of trouble. Love and care in the home make us rich in the things which count. Love and time go hand and hand. You cannot show love for a companion or a child without spending some time with that person.

We show real love for children when we trust them with a task to perform. It is carelessness to let a child grow up without feeling there are things he or she is responsible for accomplishing around the house.

Our house is on the corner of a street used as a bus stop. Many days I see a boy about ten years old walking by. In a few moments he comes back with his father. The boy has been to meet his father at the bus stop. There must be lots of love in that home for the child to be so faithful at meeting his father.

We were eating in a cafe with a young couple and their four-year-old daughter. When we bowed our heads to say a prayer of thanks before the meal, the child started to cry. Her father reached across the table and held her hand, and she was immediately quiet.

"She sits next to me at home and I always hold her hand during the blessing," her father explained.

Paul said on one occasion, "The love of Christ constraineth me." Many a son and daughter has turned away from temptation because the love of a parent constrained them. Love can move mountains; love can win battles; love keeps the world going.

Genuine love is obedient to God's will. Obedient love brings progress to the Lord's work. Parents obedient to God's will are cooperative with each other, and this provides security for the children. Obedient love brings peace in the church and the home.

## LOVE

Love is such a blessed feeling
   Which makes living so worthwhile,
For it blesses loved and lover,
   And gives life a happy style.

Love is such a precious feeling;
   'Twill enrich you every day,
As your heart in joy bestows it,
   For it's best when given away.

Love brings such a joyous feeling
   When received from friends so dear.
Love, and give out untold blessings;
   People need it, far and near.

*J. T. Bolding*

## THANK YOU, MY DEAR

I'm so grateful, dear, that you loved me,
   Enough to be my wife
And share my troubles, cares, and joys
   Through the years of life.

I thank you, dear, for what you've said;
    Your staunch encouragement
As we have walked uncertain ways:
    I know you're heaven-sent.

You've made life sweeter day by day;
    With joy you fill my years;
You've stayed beside me all the way
    And calmed my doubts and fears.

Thank you, my dear, for what you are,
    And all you mean to me;
For all those years you've been my wife
    And cared so tenderly.

*J. T. Bolding*

# 18

# *Easter Is a Time to Believe*

*I am the resurrection and the life: he that believeth in me, though he were dead, yet shall he live.—John 11:25*

> Christ the Lord is ris'n today, Alleluia!
> Sons of men and angels say, Alleluia!
> Raise your joys and triumphs high, Alleluia!
> Sing ye heavens and earth reply, Alleluia!
> *Charles Wesley*

In churches all over America at Easter time we hear beautiful Easter music—people rejoicing that Christ the Lord is risen.

Sometimes we pray and pray for something and grow discouraged because we can't seem to get an answer. We forget to wait upon the Lord's timing. One time I wanted my husband to have a new church. I felt the people in our congregation were letting him carry all the load. I prayed and prayed about it, and my husband just kept on working. Then out of the blue a church called him. It was a larger church, a church willing to work and progress. God had the time set all the while I was so impatient.

49

We arrived at our new church a week before Easter
Sunday. On Easter Sunday all the churches in the town had a
sunrise service in the city park. When we arrived at the park
almost everyone was carrying blankets, for the morning was
cold. As the service went on, the sun started up over the
horizon, and soon we were all warm and singing beautiful
Easter hymns.

People at the tomb early that first Easter morning were
cold in heart, discouraged, and unhappy. When they received
the message, "Christ is risen," the sun began to shine in their
hearts.

God can never be defeated; we must have faith and wait.
We should walk at peace in all circumstances. We are not
alone; God is with us.

We believe Christ arose, so we must go out to tell the
Easter message to others, just as the women at the tomb
spread the word. We need not be afraid: "Nay, in all these
things we are more than conquerors through him that loved
us" (Rom. 8:37).

Easter means to us that Jesus is alive forevermore. He is
still healing, comforting, saving today. Christ is not dead.

One year ago the doctors in our town told my husband
he had cancer. After many tests, they were ready to operate.
But after much prayer, my husband called and canceled the
date to enter the hospital. We went to another city and
entered a very large hospital. We both wanted a second
opinion.

We belong to a church with ten thousand members.
Many people knew J.T. because he had been on the staff of
the church for sixteen years. The church started praying for
him. Many remembered J.T.'s ministry to them in times of
sorrow and need.

After one week in the Baylor Hospital in Dallas, the

doctor gave his report: "I can find no trace of cancer, and I have thoroughly tested."

We were told later when we returned home that the day the report was given to the church, there was a great show of joy.

Christ is not dead. I believe he healed my husband.

You may have met Christ in the quiet of your home; or you may have met him in a great revival service, or even on a quiet walk in the woods on a vacation. Wherever you met Him, it proves He is not dead but was risen from the grave on that Easter morning so long ago.

If you met Christ and accepted Him as Lord and Savior, your relationship is for eternity, for good times as well as bad. The living presence of Christ in our lives helps form character and personality. He helps us fight the powers of evil.

Paul spoke of the power of the resurrection, a renewing power available to all who ask. God has power to bring men back from any kind of sin. Since Jesus came out of the tomb, "old things are passed away, behold all things become new" (II Cor. 5:17).

A poor little street urchin was adopted by a nice man and woman. He was given clean new clothes, a nice room all his own, even an allowance to spend. How wonderful for the boy. You are an orphan until you trust in Christ. Then all the glories of heaven are yours. Remember to believe at Easter.

# 19

# Mothering
# Is a Full-time Job
## (Mother's Day)

*And Pharaoh's daughter said unto her, Take this child*
*away, and nurse it for me, and I will give thee thy*
*wages.—Exod. 2:9*

*My son, hear the instruction of thy father, and forsake*
*not the law of thy mother.—Prov. 1:8*

My husband and I took a long trip in a plane. We had
never been so far from home before. We looked out the
window and could see only clouds and water below. We had
to trust the pilot to guide the plane safely to our destination.
So life is for a child born into the world. The child must trust
the father and mother to guide him safely to adulthood.

A mother's task is full time. She is with the child more
than anyone else during the first few years of life. Who can
comfort like a mother? The hurts of childhood are forgotten
when mother says a word of comfort. A child needs a mother
at all times.

Because of the cost of living we find more and more

mothers working full time and placing their children in day care centers. Oh, how much that child misses.

The evils that threaten the moral welfare of our boys and girls can't be fought to any great extent in any place but home. Many a boy and girl has been turned from evil doing because they knew of the love and confidence in the hearts of their parents.

Sometimes we read in the paper about some mother who abandoned her child or children. Just a few weeks ago two small children were found in a city in the South. They were dirty, hungry, exhausted. The mother had left them on the side of the road with a promise of ice cream when she returned. The children were too small to tell how long they had been alone but doctors judged by the dehydration of the bodies, several hours.

For every case of neglect there are thousands of stories of mothers who worked and sacrificed for their children. Such mothers deserve all our love and respect.

Washington Irving wrote, "The love of a mother is never exhausted. It never changes—it never tires—it endures through all; in good repute, in bad repute, in the face of the world's condemnation, a mother's love still lives on."

A mother has a power to live on in the hearts of her children. Because of this power she should at all times set the right example. A mother's influence is a powerful weapon. We hear very little about the mothers of great leaders, yet we know they must have had strong influence on those leaders as they were growing up.

A small boy asked his mother the definition of an angel. The mother explained that an angel was a being sent from God to minister to people in need.

Later the child was very sick with a fever. His mother seldom left his side while he was so very ill. When he became better, he looked up at his mother and said, "Mommy, you are an angel."

Walter Russell Bowie wrote, "For the child's full growth in happiness, in confidence, and in serenity of soul, the gentle spirit of his mother is more powerful than all the world beside."

### MY ALTAR

I have worshiped in churches and chapels,
I've prayed in the busy street,
I have sought my God and found Him
Where the waves of His ocean beat;
I have knelt in the silent forest
In the shade of some ancient tree,
But the dearest of all my altars
Was raised at my mother's knee.

*Unknown*

### NOBODY KNOWS BUT MOTHER

How many lunches for Tommy and Sam?
  Nobody knows but Mother,
Cookies and apples and blackberry jam—
  Nobody knows but Mother.
Nourishing dainties for every "sweet tooth,"
Toddling Dottie or dignified Ruth—
How much love sweetens the labor, forsooth?
  Nobody knows but Mother.

How many cares does a mother's heart know?
  Nobody knows but Mother.
How many joys from her mother love flow?
  Nobody knows but Mother.
How many prayers for each little white bed?
How many tears for her babies has she shed?
How many kisses for each curly head?
  Nobody knows but Mother.

*Unknown*

# 20

# *Thanksgiving Miracles*

*Master, we have toiled all the night, and have taken nothing: nevertheless at thy word I will let down the net. And when they had this done, they inclosed a great multitude of fishes: and their net brake.—Luke 5:5-6*

Several years ago at Thanksgiving time a story was published in our local newspaper. A busy druggist one day found a little girl about six years old in his store. "What do you want?" he asked.

Holding out her hand to his she poured out twenty-seven pennies. She said, "I want to buy a miracle."

When the druggist, a fine, active Christian, questioned the child further, he found that the little girl had a younger brother who had something wrong with his back. He could not grow and develop normally. A friend visiting the family one day said, "Why don't you take the boy to a good doctor; maybe he could be helped."

But her mother had answered, "We have no money for anything like an expensive doctor."

The friend replied, "Then it will take a miracle to make him walk."

The druggist went to his pastor and the miracle was bought. His church furnished the money to send the child to the Scottish Rite Hospital for Crippled Children in Dallas.

The age of miracles is not dead. God can use a small girl who is willing to give all she has for a miracle.

There will be some adverse circumstances in life. Yet we can meet those crises better if we are secure in God's love, if we are thankful for each new day and its blessings.

As Thanksgiving Day drew near the second grade pupils at one school began to make big plans. All except Billy were excited and enthusiastic.

One day the teacher singled Billy out: "Are you going to have a nice Thanksgiving?"

"Well, Mommy said if we even have meat to eat on Thanksgiving, the Lord will have to provide it."

At the close of the school day, the teacher looked at her file on Billy. She found that he had a mother with no husband and three school age children. As she looked over the file she thought of several organizations in town who distributed baskets on the day before Thanksgiving. She also noted the name of the church Billy's mother belonged to. After a few phone calls the teacher was assured Billy's family would have food for the holiday.

When the holidays were over the young teacher was eager to hear about all the children's activities. She called on Billy first.

"We had a wonderful Thanksgiving. The Lord was busy; He didn't come but He sent the church people with a big basket."

## THE THANKFUL HEART

For all that God in mercy sends—
For health and children, home, and friends;
For comfort in the time of need,
For every kindly word or deed,
For happy thoughts and holy talk,
For guidance in our daily walk—
In everything give thanks!

For beauty in this world of ours,
For verdant grass and lovely flowers,
For songs of birds, for hum of bees,
For the refreshing summer breeze,
For hill and plain, for stream and wood,
For the great ocean's mighty flood—
In everything give thanks!

For the sweet sleep which comes with night,
For the returning morning light,
For the bright sun that shines on high,
For the stars glittering in the sky—
For these and everything we see,
O Lord, our heart we lift to Thee;
In everything give thanks!

*Unknown*

# 21

# *Day of Wonder*
## *(Christmas)*

*For unto us a child is born, unto us a son is given: and the government shall be upon his shoulder: and his name shall be called Wonderful, Counsellor, The mighty God, The everlasting Father, The Prince of Peace.—Isa. 9:6*

*And when they were come into the house, they saw the young child with Mary his mother, and fell down, and worshiped him: and when they had opened their treasures, they presented unto him gifts; gold, frankincense, and myrrh.—Matt. 2:11*

As Christmas drew near this year, my husband and I felt a little let down. Our three children and their families were not coming for Christmas. Some of them would come to our daughter's home twenty-five miles away on the weekend before Christmas. What would Christmas be without a big noisy crowd?

Feeling sorry for myself, I unpacked one box of decorations. In the box I found a holder with eight electric candles.

58

"I'll put these candles in the front window and light the way for those passing by," I mused. "No one will know we are not having a wonderful day."

I thought of the day of wonder when the wise men of old followed the star and arrived at the house where the baby Jesus was and presented Him with gifts. I thought of the reason for Christmas. I had no reason to be selfish. I needed to give.

When I took time to stop feeling sorry for myself because the children were not coming, I started thinking of others and being happy.

I pictured the different children and grandchildren and knew that in their own way each would have a wonderful day. They would read the Christmas story, sing a few songs, and tell what special blessings the year had brought to them. All would have an overabundance of gifts. My prayer was that all would be well and happy.

My great thanksgiving was that all my dear ones who were old enough had known that wonderful day when they met the Savior. All were safe in His kingdom. What greater gift could we have than salvation!

As I looked at my joys and blessings through the magnifying glass of happiness, the place we would be or the people we would be with did not seem so important. I realized God magnifies his kindness all the days if we let him rule our lives. We just forget at times to look and see His blessings.

My friend wanted a ring for Christmas. She had been married twenty years and never had a ring as a gift from her husband. She just knew she would get the ring this particular Christmas.

As her family received their gifts one by one, she heard cries of delight and joy, but she did not receive the small package she had hoped to get.

"Mother, where is your gift?" one of the children asked.

"Here they are," she said as she showed them place mats, hose, a vase, and other odds and ends.

"Daddy, where is Mother's gift?" the child asked.

The husband reached in his pocket and brought out the long awaited gift. He had been so excited over the toys and games he had forgotten the most important gift of all.

The wonderful day was a little spoiled for all the family because they had expected there to be such a great moment of joy when their mother received the ring.

Before we condemn the seemingly thoughtless husband, let us look at our own lives. How many times do we get so excited over "things" at this wonderful season that we forget the greatest gift of all—Christ our Lord?

Erin, a five-year-old who lives across the street, brought us a pan of rolls for Christmas. As she stood in the door so pure and sweet our hearts overflowed with joy. Our gift to her was not large or expensive, but she said, "Thank you, Boldings." It was not the size of the gift but the joy of knowing she was very important to us that made her happy.

We are God's children; we are important to Him. He wants every day to be a day of wonder and grace for us.

### TRUE GIVING
The spirit of true giving was
    At Christmas time begun
Long, long ago, by God Himself
    When He gave Christ His Son.

The dearest joy that we can get,
    When from our hearts we give,
Is just to see our gifts received
    By hearts both glad and sensitive.

The meanest thing a man can do
To God, who gave His son,
Is to reject his wondrous gift
And His great love to shun.

*J. T. Bolding*